Lights in the Snow

Level 4+
Blue+

Helpful Hints for Reading at Home

The graphemes (written letters) and phonemes (units of sound) used throughout this series are aligned with Letters and Sounds. This offers a consistent approach to learning whether reading at home or in the classroom.

THIS BLUE+ BOOK BAND SERVES AS AN INTRODUCTION TO PHASE 5. EACH BOOK IN THIS BAND USES ALL PHONEMES LEARNED UP TO PHASE 4, WHILE INTRODUCING ONE PHASE 5 PHONEME. HERE IS A LIST OF PHONEMES FOR THIS PHASE, WITH THE NEW PHASE 5 PHONEME. AN EXAMPLE OF THE PRONUNCIATION CAN BE FOUND IN BRACKETS.

Phase 3			
j (jug)	v (van)	w (wet)	x (fox)
y (yellow)	z (zoo)	zz (buzz)	qu (quick)
ch (chip)	sh (shop)	th (thin/then)	ng (ring)
ai (rain)	ee (feet)	igh (night)	oa (boat)
oo (boot/look)	ar (farm)	or (for)	ur (hurt)
ow (cow)	oi (coin)	ear (dear)	air (fair)
ure (sure)	er (corner)		

New Phase 5 Phoneme	ow (window, blow, snow)

HERE ARE SOME WORDS WHICH YOUR CHILD MAY FIND TRICKY.

Phase 4 Tricky Words			
said	were	have	there
like	little	so	one
do	when	some	out
come	what		

TOP TIPS FOR HELPING YOUR CHILD TO READ:

- Allow children time to break down unfamiliar words into units of sound and then encourage children to string these sounds together to create the word.

- Encourage your child to point out any focus phonics when they are used.

- Read through the book more than once to grow confidence.

- Ask simple questions about the text to assess understanding.

- Encourage children to use illustrations as prompts.

This book introduces the phoneme /ow/ and is a Blue+ Level 4+ book band.

Lights in the Snow

Written by
Madeline Tyler

Illustrated by
Amy Li

Alba is in her hut. She is on her own and she is sad.

It is dark, but Alba needs to get up.
There is a lot to do!

From her window she can see the snow.
Alba shivers.

Alba checks her plans. She grabs her coat, her hat and her bag. She is off!

The wind is howling and blowing the snow.

Alba stomps in her big snow boots.
The wind is strong, but she will not slip!

The wind blows. With one big gust, there is snow on Alba!

Alba jumps up and down and blows the snow off. Alba must go on.

Alba is in the trees to look for wood. She checks her plans.

She needs lots of wood. It is in her bag, and she is off.

There is a lot of snow and the wind is strong. Alba is slow.

The wind blows hard. Alba is down in the snow!

Alba is low and the trees are high.
The wind blows and howls.

The shadows are long and dark. "I do not like this," sobs Alba.

Alba is sitting below the trees. She looks up and sees a glow.

She rests on her elbows to see the yellows and pinks and greens.

Alba must not be afraid of the shadows. She must get back and finish her job!

Alba follows the glowing lights. They show her how to get back to her hut.

Alba drags her bag with wood and sticks in. A trail is left in the snow.

The wind is still blowing, but Alba is there! Now Alba is below the glowing lights.

Alba drops the wood. She starts off low and stacks it up.

The stacks of wood look like huts!
Some are big and some are little.

The huts are for Alba and all of her pals.

They have hats and coats and pillows and mugs.

Alba and her pals look up at the show.
The lights flow like rivers and rainbows.

Alba is with her pals. She is not on her own.

Lights in the Snow

1) Why do you think Alba is sad at the beginning of the story?

2) What is Alba looking for in the trees?
   a) Wood
   b) Leaves
   c) Flowers

3) What colours does Alba see in the sky?

4) What animals does Alba build huts for?

5) How do you think Alba feels at the end of the story? Why?

©2022 **BookLife Publishing Ltd.**
King's Lynn, Norfolk PE30 4LS

ISBN 978-1-80155-171-7

All rights reserved. Printed in Poland.
A catalogue record for this book is available from the British Library.

Lights in the Snow
Written by Madeline Tyler
Illustrated by Amy Li

An Introduction to BookLife Readers...

Our Readers have been specifically created in line with the London Institute of Education's approach to book banding and are phonetically decodable and ordered to support each phase of the Letters and Sounds document.

Each book has been created to provide the best possible reading and learning experience. Our aim is to share our love of books with children, providing both emerging readers and prolific page-turners with beautiful books that are guaranteed to provoke interest and learning, regardless of ability.

BOOK BAND GRADED using the Institute of Education's approach to levelling.

PHONETICALLY DECODABLE supporting each phase of Letters and Sounds.

EXERCISES AND QUESTIONS to offer reinforcement and to ascertain comprehension.

BEAUTIFULLY ILLUSTRATED to inspire and provoke engagement, providing a variety of styles for the reader to enjoy whilst reading through the series.

**AUTHOR INSIGHT:
MADELINE TYLER**

Native to Norfolk, England, Madeline Tyler's intelligence and professionalism can be felt in the 50-plus books that she has written for BookLife Publishing. A graduate of Queen Mary University of London with a 1st Class degree in Comparative Literature, she also received a University Volunteering Award for helping children to read at a local school.

When she was a child, Madeline enjoyed playing the violin, and she now relaxes through yoga and reading books!

This book introduces the phoneme /ow/ and is a Blue+ Level 4+ book band.